Baby Turtles at the Zoo

Cecelia H. Brannon

Enslow Publishing
101 W. 23rd Street
Suite 240
New York, NY 10011
USA
enslow.com

Published in 2016 by Enslow Publishing, LLC.
101 W. 23rd Street, Suite 240, New York, NY 10011

Library of Congress Cataloging-in-Publication Data

Brannon, Cecelia H.
  Baby turtles at the zoo / by Cecelia H. Brannon.
    p. cm. — (All about baby zoo animals)
  Includes bibliographical references and index.
  ISBN 978-0-7660-7160-5 (library binding)
  ISBN 978-0-7660-7158-2 (pbk.)
  ISBN 978-0-7660-7159-9 (6-pack)
  1. Turtles — Infancy — Juvenile literature. 2. Zoo animals — Juvenile literature. I. Brannon, Cecelia
H. II. Title.
  QL666.C5 B73 2016
  598.1'3—d23

Printed in the United States of America

To Our Readers: We have done our best to make sure all website addresses in this book were active and appropriate when we went to press. However, the author and the publisher have no control over and assume no liability for the material available on those websites or on any websites they may link to. Any comments or suggestions can be sent by e-mail to customerservice@enslow.com.

Photos Credits: Cover © iStockphoto.com/worakit_; p. 1 NaturePL/NaturePL/SuperStock; pp. 4–5
© iStockphoto.com/ filo; p. 6 © iStockphoto.com/Jamie Farrant; pp. 3 (center), 8 Animals Animals/
Animals Animals/SuperStock; p. 10 © iStockphoto.com/Thomas_Zsebok_Images; pp. 3 (right), 12
fztommy/Shutterstock.com; p. 14 Dmitry_Tsveltkov/Shutterstock.com; p. 16 © TWRC Wildlife Center;
pp. 3 (left), 18 Elena Kouptsova-Vasic/Shutterstock.com; p. 20 john a. shaw/Shutterstock.com; p. 22 Jay
Ondreicka/Shutterstock.com.

Contents

Words to Know

bale   hatchling   webbed

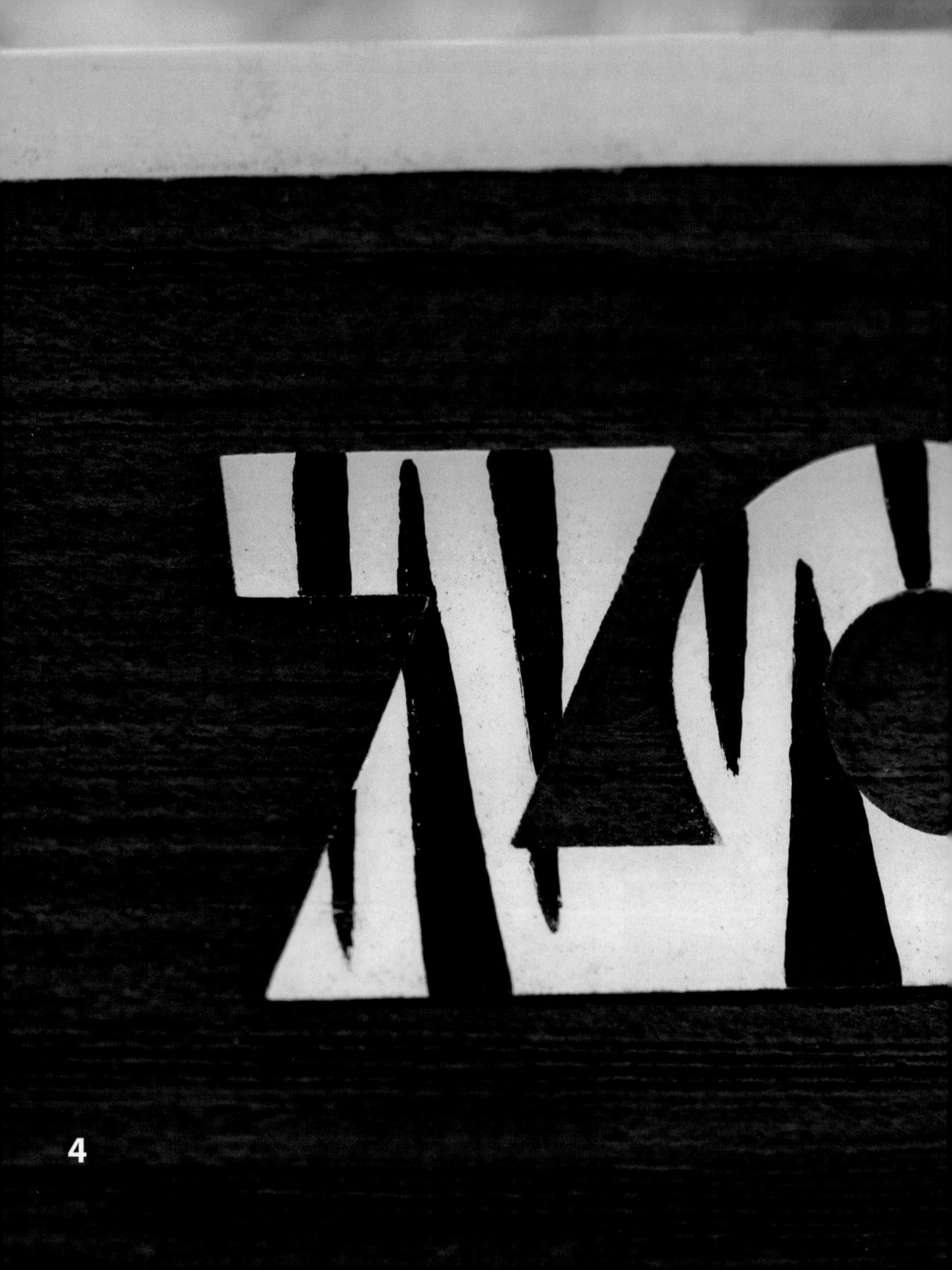

Who lives at the zoo?

A baby turtle lives at the zoo!

A baby turtle is called a hatchling. It hatches from an egg.

A turtle hatchling can be many colors. But most are green or brown. They have shells on their backs that protect them.

A turtle hatchling has webbed feet. This helps it swim.

A turtle hatchling spends most of its life in water. But it likes to climb out onto logs or rocks to lay in the sun.

A turtle hatchling eats plants and animals. The zookeeper feeds it fruit, yams, lettuce, worms, and small fish like goldfish or minnows.

A turtle hatchling lives in the zoo with other turtles. A group of turtles is called a bale.

Some turtle hatchlings can pull their heads into their shells. This keeps them safe from danger.

You can see a turtle hatchling at the zoo!

Read More

Hanson, Anders. *Sea Turtle*. Edina, MN: ABDO, 2014.

Marsh, Laura. *National Geographic Readers: Turtles*. Washington, DC: National Geographic Children's Books, 2016.

Websites

Science Kids: Fun Turtle Facts for Kids
sciencekids.co.nz/sciencefacts/animals/turtle.html

National Geographic Kids: Leatherback Sea Turtles
kids.nationalgeographic.com/content/kids/en_US/animals/leatherback-sea-turtle/

Index

Guided Reading Level: D
Guided Reading Leveling System is based on the guidelines recommended by Fountas and Pinnell.

Word Count: 146